Usborne

my very first Castles book

Illustrated by Lee Cosgrove
Written by Dr. Abigail Wheatley
Designed by Alice Reese

CASTLE TIMES

Hundreds of years ago, there were lots of wars and a lot of fighting. Kings and lords needed somewhere safe to live. So, they built castles.

Guards hide behind these battlements.

Strong towers

Guards can shoot arrows out of these slits.

I'm safe in here!

Moat filled with water

This drawbridge can be pulled up so no one can get in.

Great tower

Attackers can't get in through these tiny windows.

Strong gate

Thick walls

Deep ditch

Narrow bridge

Fighting knights

Sword

War horse

Flag

Shield

3

CASTLE PEOPLE

Only kings and queens or important lords and ladies had their own castles. They lived there with their families and helpers. Look out for all these people as you read this book.

A lord and lady and their children

Attendants who take care of the lord, lady and children

Find me on every double page!

Knights and fighters who guard the castle

Officials who take care of the lord's business

Priests who are in charge of the chapel

Officials who serve meals

Entertainers

Workers who take care
of the castle animals

Servants who run the kitchen

Handymen who fix the castle

Servants who clean the
castle and fetch and carry

BUILDING A CASTLE

Sometimes it took many years to build a castle, especially a big one. There were lots of different jobs to be done, and lots of people to do them.

1. Finding a site

2. Digging a ditch

3. Cutting stones

4. Carrying stones

5. Mixing mortar

6. Building walls

7. Scaffolding

8. Raising stones

9. Taking a break

10. Shaping windows

11. Building battlements

12. Making roofs

13. Making a drawbridge

14. Painting

15. Finished!

Inside a Castle

Pulling up
the portcullis

Door

Bed chamber

Chest

Bed

Taking a bath

Sweeping

Toilet

Guard room

Spears

Guards

Playing dice

Chapel

Priest

Praying

Dungeon

Prisoners

Rat

Most of the walls
have been cut
away, so you can
see inside.

A FEAST

Every castle had a big, busy kitchen, full of cooks.
Some days, there was a huge feast in the great hall
of the castle, so the kitchen was busier than ever.

Fireplace

Roasting meat

Turning a spit

Boiling stew

Herbs

Plucking feathers

Making pastry

Pastry castle

Head cook

Washing dishes

Grinding spices

Chopping vegetables

Box of spices

Roast peacock

A DAY IN A CASTLE

4 o'clock — Servants starting work

5 o'clock — Officials starting work

6 o'clock — Opening the drawbridge

4 o'clock — Another service in chapel

3 o'clock — "Cheers!" — Entertaining guests

2 o'clock — Business meetings

5 o'clock — Supper

6 o'clock — Entertainments

7 o'clock — Counting money

8 o'clock — Service in chapel

9 o'clock — Breakfast

1 o'clock — Nap time

11 o'clock — Lunch

10 o'clock — Going hunting

8 o'clock — Bedtime for lord and lady

9 o'clock — Shutting the drawbridge

10 o'clock — Bedtime for servants

CASTLE ANIMALS

Some animals had important jobs to do, so they lived in castles too. Horses had stables, dogs had kennels and there were even perches for trained birds.

Stable

Castle cat

Bringing food

Horses

Cleaning

Saddles

Grooming

Kennel

Dogs

Drinking water

Outdoor area

High perch

Low perch

This buildin is for traine birds.

Bandaging an injured dog

This trained bird is a falcon.

Outdoor perch

Partridge

Hare

Some large birds were trained to catch smaller birds and animals for people to eat.

People rode horses on journeys...

when they went hunting...

or when they went to battle.

Hunting horn

Boar spear

Leash

These dogs are bloodhounds.

Wild boar

Dogs helped to hunt animals such as deer and wild boar, for people in the castle to eat.

AROUND A CASTLE

Outside a castle's walls, there was a lot going on. Castle servants often lived in a nearby village. There were fields, mills for grinding flour and even fish ponds.

Church

People come here to drink ale.

The castle cook lives here.

Village

Stocks

Thief being punished

Getting water from a well

Wheat is ground into flour at this mill.

The castle gardener lives here.

Pigs

Castle

Forest for hunting

Jousting area

Castle gardens

Sheep

Cows

Food for the castle is grown here.

Harvesting wheat

Orchard

Catching fish for the castle

Geese

17

Knights

Knights were warriors trained to fight on horseback. They wore metal suits to protect them and had different weapons to fight with.

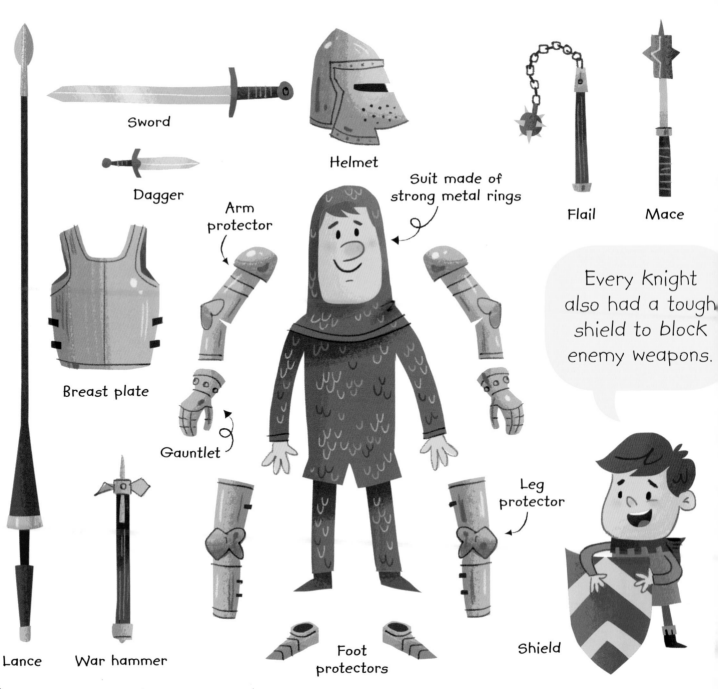

Sword

Dagger

Helmet

Suit made of strong metal rings

Flail

Mace

Arm protector

Breast plate

Gauntlet

Every Knight also had a tough shield to block enemy weapons.

Leg protector

Lance

War hammer

Foot protectors

Shield

19

Becoming a Knight

It took 10 years of training to become a knight. A boy started when he was around 7 years old. At first he was called a page and had to fetch and carry. Then, he became a squire and learned fighting and lots of other skills.

1. Fetching and carrying

2. Polishing weapons

3. Learning to ride

4. Playing chess

5. Battle training

6. Reading

7. Horse riding

8. Sword skills

9. Dressing a Knight

10. Keeping fit

11. Handling a lance

12. Music and dancing

13. Hunting

14. Helping in battles

15. Finally becoming a Knight

JOUSTING

Sometimes Knights had pretend fights. They tried to knock each other off their horses with poles called lances. This was called jousting. Crowds of people watched, and some of them had their own pretend fights, too.

Tents

Lords and ladies

Sir Simon

Sir Robert

Sir Simon's horse

Watching

Hot pies!

Sir Robert's squire

Lance

Wrestling match

Sir Simon has lost.

Sir Robert wins a prize...

and keeps Sir Simon's horse.

Under attack!

Sometimes, enemies attacked a castle.
They tried all kinds of ways to get in.
But the people inside fought back.

SWISH!

Tents

WHOOSH!

Trebuchet

Loading rocks

Swimming

Battering ram

Firing arrows

CASTLE PASTIMES

When there was no fighting to do, lords, ladies and their children found different ways of relaxing in and around their castles.

Smelling flowers

Playing tag

Walking in the garden

Playing a board game

Talking

Doll

Hobby horse

Listening to stories

Embroidery

Playing music and dancing

Visiting friends   Writing letters   Reading books

Watching plays

FROM CASTLE TO CASTLE

Kings and very rich lords sometimes had lots of castles. They went from one to another, spending a few weeks at each. And they took EVERYTHING with them.

Wine

Kitchen equipment

Jewels

Spices

Books

Bowls and cups

Clothes

Board games

Money

Bedding

Tapestries

Rugs

Weapons

Clothes

Jewels

Spices

Kitchen equipment

Servants

Wine

Tapestries

Bedding

Money

Officials

Queen and ladies

Priest

Guards

Carriage

Castle

Squires

Knights

King

Falcon

Horses

Dogs

29

THE STORY OF CASTLES

Over 1,000 years ago

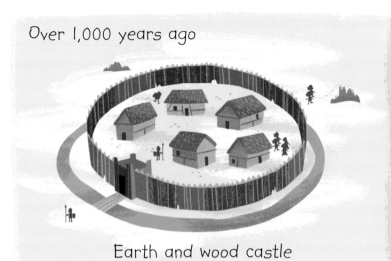

Earth and wood castle

1,000 years ago

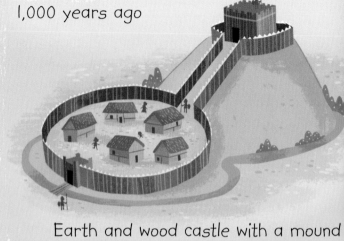

Earth and wood castle with a mound

700 years ago

Castle with two very strong rings of walls

800 years ago

Castle with two rings of walls

550 years ago

Castle wrecked by new weapons

300 years ago

Abandoned castle

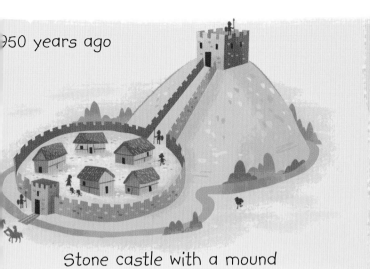

950 years ago

Stone castle with a mound

900 years ago

Stone castle with a great tower

830 years ago

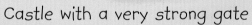

Castle with a very strong gate

850 years ago

Stone castle without a great tower

Today

Visiting a castle

INDEX

Series Editor: Ruth Brocklehurst   Series Designer: Josephine Thompson